Thomas Wentworth Higginson

Short Studies of American Authors

Thomas Wentworth Higginson

Short Studies of American Authors

ISBN/EAN: 9783337279332

Printed in Europe, USA, Canada, Australia, Japan

Cover: Foto ©Thomas Meinert / pixelio.de

More available books at **www.hansebooks.com**

SHORT STUDIES

OF

AMERICAN AUTHORS.

BY

THOMAS WENTWORTH HIGGINSON.

————————

BOSTON:
LEE AND SHEPARD, PUBLISHERS.
NEW YORK:
CHARLES T. DILLINGHAM.
1880.

PREFACE.

THESE brief papers were originally published in "The Literary World" (Boston), and are here reprinted in a revised form, with some additions.

CAMBRIDGE, MASS., Dec. 1, 1879.

TABLE OF CONTENTS.

SHORT STUDIES

OF

AMERICAN AUTHORS.

———•◦•———

HAWTHORNE.

I DO not know when I have been more surprised
than on being asked, the other day, whether
Hawthorne was not physically very small. It
seemed at the moment utterly unconceivable that
he should have been any thing less than the sombre
and commanding personage he was. Ellery Channing well describes him as a

> " Tall, compacted figure, ably strung,
> To urge the Indian chase, or point the way."

One can imagine any amount of positive energy
— that of Napoleon Bonaparte, for instance — as
included within a small physical frame. But the
self-contained purpose of Hawthorne, the large
resources, the waiting power, — these seem to the
imagination to imply an ample basis of physical
life ; and certainly his stately and noble port is

inseparable, in my memory, from these charac-
teristics.

Vivid as this impression is, I yet saw him but
twice, and never spoke to him. I first met him on
a summer morning, in Concord, as he was walking
along the road near the Old Manse, with his wife
by his side, and a noble-looking baby-boy in a
little wagon which the father was pushing. I remember him as tall, firm, and strong in bearing;
his wife looked pensive and dreamy, as she indeed
was, then and always; the child was Julian, then
known among the neighbors as "the Prince."
When I passed, Hawthorne lifted upon me his
great gray eyes, with a look too keen to seem indifferent, too shy to be sympathetic — and that was
all. But it comes back to memory like that one
glimpse of Shelley which Browning describes, and
which he likens to the day when he found an
eagle's feather.

Again I met Hawthorne at one of the sessions
of a short-lived literary club; and I recall the
imperturbable dignity and patience with which he
sat through a vexatious discussion, whose details
seemed as much dwarfed by his presence as if he
had been a statue of Olympian Zeus. After his
death I had a brief but intimate acquaintance with
that rare person, Mrs. Hawthorne; and with one

still more finely organized, and born to a destiny of sadness, — their elder daughter. I have staid at "The Wayside," occupying a room in the small tower built by Hawthorne, and containing his lofty and then deserted study, which still bore upon its wall the Tennysonian motto, "There is no joy but calm," — this having been inscribed, however, not by himself, but by his son. It is not my purpose to dwell upon the facts of private life; and these circumstances are mentioned only because it is well to know at what angle of incidence any critic has been touched by the personality of a great author.

Perhaps it always appears to men, as they grow older, that there was rather more of positive force and vitality in their own generation and among their immediate predecessors, than among those just coming on the stage. This may be the reason why there seems to me a perpetual sense of grasp and vigor in Hawthorne's most delicate sketches; while much of the most graceful writing now done in America makes no such impression, but either seems like dainty confectionery, or like carving minute heads on cherry-stones. In England the tendency is just now to the opposite fault, — to a distrust of all nice attention to form in writing, as being necessarily a weakness. Hawthorne happily escaped both these dangerous alternatives; and, indeed, it is hard to see that his genius was much affected by his surroundings, after all. He had, to be sure, the conscientious fidelity of Puritanism in his veins, a thing equally important for literature and for life : without it he might have lavished and wasted himself like Poe. He had what Emerson once described as "the still living merit of the oldest New-England families;"[1] he had moreover the unexhausted wealth of the Puritan traditions, — a wealth to which only he and Whittier have as yet done any justice. The value of the material to be found in contemporary American life he never fully recognized ; but he was the first person to see that we really have, for romantic purposes, a past ; two hundred years being really quite enough to constitute antiquity. This was what his " environment " gave him, and this was much.

But, after all, his artistic standard was his own : there was nobody except Irving to teach him any thing in that way ; and Irving's work lay rather on the surface, and could be no model for Hawthorne's. Yet from the time when the latter began to write for " The Token," at twenty-three, his powers of execution, as of thought, appear to have been full-grown. The quiet ease is there, the pellucid language, the haunting quality : these gifts were born

1 " The Dial." iii., 101.

in him ; we cannot trace them back to any period of formation. And when we consider the degree to which they were developed, how utterly unfilled remains his peculiar throne ; how powerless would be the accumulated literary forces of London, for instance, at this day, to produce a single page that could possibly be taken for Hawthorne's, — we see that there must, after all, be such a thing as literary art, and that he must represent one of the very highest types of artist.

Through Hawthorne's journals we trace the mental impulses by which he first obtained his themes. Then in his unfinished " Septimius Felton," — fortunately unfinished for this purpose, — we see his plastic imagination at work in shaping the romance ; we watch him trying one mode of treatment, then modifying it by another; always aiming at the main point, but sometimes pausing to elaborate the details, and at other times dismissing them to be worked out at leisure. There hangs before me, as I write, a photograph of one of Raphael's rough sketches, drawn on the back of a letter : there is a group of heads, then another group on a different scale ; you follow the shifting mood of the artist's mind ; and so it is in reading " Septimius Felton." In all Hawthorne's completed works, the pencilling is rubbed out, and every trace of the preliminary labor has disappeared.

One of the most characteristic of Hawthorne's literary methods is his habitual use of guarded under-statements and veiled hints. It is not a sign of weakness, but of conscious strength, when he surrounds each delineation with a sort of penumbra, takes you into his counsels, offers hypotheses, as, "May it not have been?" or, "Shall we not rather say?" and sometimes, like a conjurer, urges particularly upon you the card he does not intend you to accept. He seems not quite to know whether Arthur Dimmesdale really had a fiery scar on his breast, or what finally became of Miriam and her lover. He will gladly share with you any information he possesses, and, indeed, has several valuable hints to offer; but that is all. The result is, that you place yourself by his side to look with him at his characters, and gradually share with him the conviction that they must be real. Then, when he has you thus in possession, he calls your attention to the profound ethics involved in the tale, and yet does it so gently that you never think of the moral as being obtrusive.

All this involved a trait which was always supreme in him, — a marvellous self-control. He had by nature that gift which the musical composer Jomelli went to a teacher to seek, — "the art of not being embarrassed by his own ideas." Mrs.

Hawthorne told me that her husband grappled alone all winter with " The Scarlet Letter," and came daily from his study with a knot in his forehead ; and yet his self-mastery was so complete that every sentence would seem to have crystallized in an atmosphere of perfect calm. We see the value of this element in his literary execution, when we turn from it to that of an author so great as Lowell, for instance, and see him often entangled and weighed down by his own rich thoughts, his style being overcrowded by the very wealth it bears. Hawthorne never needed Italic letters to distribute his emphasis, never a footnote for assistance. There was no conception so daring that he shrank from attempting it ; and none that he could not so master as to state it, if he pleased, in terms of monosyllables.

For all these merits he paid one high and inexorable penalty, — the utter absence of all immediate or dazzling success. His publisher, Goodrich, tells us, in his " Reminiscences,"[1] that Hawthorne and Willis began to write together in " The Token," in 1827, and that the now-forgotten Willis " rose rapidly to fame," while Hawthorne's writings " did not attract the slightest attention." The only recognition of his merits that I have been able to find in the contemporary criticism of those early

[1] Vol. ii., p 269.

years is in "The New-England Magazine" for
October, 1834, where he is classed approvingly
with those who were then considered the eminent writers of the day, — Miss Sedgwick, Miss
Leslie, Verplanck, Greenwood, and John Neal.
"To them," the critic says, "we may add an
anonymous author of some of the most delicate
and beautiful prose ever published this side of
the Atlantic, — the author of 'The Gentle Boy.' "[1]
For twenty years he continued to be, according
to his own statement, "the obscurest man of
letters in America." Goodrich testifies that it
was almost impossible to find a publisher for
"Twice-Told Tales" in 1837, and I can myself
remember how limited a circle greeted the re-
print in the enlarged edition of 1841. When
Poe, about 1846, wrote patronizingly of Hawthorne, he added, "It was never the fashion, until
lately, to speak of him in any summary of our best
authors."[2] Whittier once told me that when he
himself had obtained, with some difficulty, in 1847,
the insertion of one of Hawthorne's sketches in
"The National Era," the latter said quietly,
"There is not much market for my wares." It has
always seemed to me the greatest triumph of his

[1] New-England Magazine, October, 1834, p. 331.
[2] Poe's Works (ed. 1853), iii. 189.

genius, not that he bore poverty without a murmur,
— for what right has a literary man, who can command his time and his art, to sigh after the added
enjoyments of mere wealth?— but that he went on
doing work of such a quality for an audience so
small or so indifferent.

Whether more immediate applause would have
modified the result, it is now impossible to say.
Having so much, why should we ask for more?
An immediate popularity might possibly have
added a little more sunshine to his thought, a
few drops of redder blood to his style; thus
averting the only criticism that can ever be justly
made on either. Yet this very privation has made
him a nobler and tenderer figure in literary history;
and a source of more tonic influence for young
writers, through all coming time. The popular
impression of Hawthorne as a shy and lonely
man, gives but a part of the truth. When we
think of him as reading "The Scarlet Letter" to
his sympathetic wife, until she pressed her hands
to her ears, and could bear no more; or when we
imagine him as playing with his children so gayly
that one of them told me "there never was such
a playmate in all the world,"— we may feel that he
had, after all, the very best that earth can give, and
all our regrets seem only an impertinence.

POE.

IT happens to us rarely in our lives to come consciously into the presence of that extraordinary miracle we call genius. Among the many literary persons whom I have happened to meet, at home or abroad, there are not half a dozen who have left an irresistible sense of this rare quality; and, among these few, Poe stands next to Hawthorne in the vividness of personal impression he produced. I saw him but once; and it was on that celebrated occasion, in 1845, when he startled Boston by substituting his boyish production, "Al Aaraaf," for the more serious poem which he was to have delivered before the Lyceum. There was much curiosity to see him; for his prose-writings had been eagerly read, at least among college-students, and his poems were just beginning to excite still greater attention. After a rather solid and very partisan address by Caleb Cushing, then just returned from his Chinese embassy, the poet was introduced. I distinctly recall his face, with its ample forehead, brilliant eyes, and narrowness• of nose and chin; an essentially ideal face, not noble, yet any thing but coarse; with the look of over-sensitiveness which when uncontrolled may prove more debasing than coarseness. It was a face to rivet one's attention in any crowd, yet a face that no one would feel safe in loving. It is not perhaps strange that I find or fancy in the portrait of Charles Baudelaire, Poe's French admirer and translator, some of the traits that are indelibly associated with that one glimpse of Poe.

I remember that when introduced he stood with a sort of shrinking before the audience, and then began in a thin, tremulous, hardly musical voice, an apology for his poem, and a deprecation of the expected criticism of the Boston public; reiterating this in a sort of persistent, querulous way, which did not seem like satire, but impressed me at the time as nauseous flattery. It was not then generally known, nor was it established for a long time after, — even when he had himself asserted it, — that the poet was himself born in Boston; and no one can now tell, perhaps, what was the real feeling behind the apparently sycophantic attitude. When, at the end, he abruptly began the recitation of his rather perplexing poem, everybody looked thor-

oughly mystified. The verses had long since been
printed in his youthful volume, and had re-appeared
within a few days, if I mistake not, in Wiley &
Putnam's edition of his poems; and they produced no very distinct impression on the audience
until Poe began to read the maiden's song in the
second part. Already his tones had been soften-
ing to a finer melody than at first, and when he
came to the verse, —

> " Ligeia ! Ligeia,
>   My beautiful one !
> Whose harshest idea
>   Will to melody run,
> Oh ! is it thy will
>   On the breezes to toss ?
> Or capriciously still
>   Like the lone albatross
> Incumbent on night
>   (As she on the air)
> To keep watch with delight
>   On the harmony there ? "

his voice seemed attenuated to the finest golden
thread ; the audience became hushed, and, as it
were, breathless ; there seemed no life in the hall
but his ; and every syllable was accentuated with
such delicacy, and sustained with such sweetness,
as I never heard equalled by other lips. When
the lyric ended, it was like the ceasing of the

gypsy's chant in Browning's "Flight of the Duchess;" and I remember nothing more, except that in walking back to Cambridge my comrades and I felt that we had been under the spell of some wizard. Indeed, I feel much the same in the retrospect, to this day.

The melody did not belong, in this case, to the poet's voice alone: it was already in the words. His verse, when he was willing to give it natural utterance, was like that of Coleridge in rich sweetness, and like that was often impaired by theories of structure and systematic experiments in metre. Never in American literature, I think, was such a fountain of melody flung into the air as when "Lenore" first appeared in "The Pioneer;" and never did fountain so drop downward as when Poe re-arranged it in its present form. The irregular measure had a beauty as original as that of "Christabel;" and the lines had an ever-varying, ever-lyrical cadence of their own, until their author himself took them, and cramped them into couplets. What a change from

> "*Peccavimus!*
> But rave not thus!
> And let the solemn song
> Go up to God so mournfully that *she* may feel no wrong!"

to the amended version, portioned off in regular lengths, thus : —

" Peccavimus ! but rave not thus ! and let a Sabbath song
  Go up to God so solemnly, the dead may feel no wrong."

Or worse yet, when he introduced that tedious jingle of slightly varied repetition which in later year reached its climax in lines like these : —

" Till the fair and gentle Eulalie became my blushing bride,
  Till the yellow-haired young Eulalie became my smiling
    bride."

This trick, caught from Poe, still survives in our literature ; made more permanent, perhaps, by the success of his " Raven." This poem, which made him popular, seems to me far inferior to some of his earlier and slighter effusions ; as those exquisite verses " To Helen," which are among our American classics, and have made

" The glory that was Greece,
  And the grandeur that was Rome,"

a permanent phrase in our language.

Poe's place in purely imaginative prose-writing is as unquestionable as Hawthorne's. He even succeeded, which Hawthorne did not, in penetrating the artistic indifference of the French mind ; and it was a substantial triumph, when we consider that Baudelaire put himself or his friends to the trouble of translating even the prolonged platitudes of "Eureka," and the wearisome narrative of "Arthur Gordon Pym." Neither Poe nor Hawthorne has ever been fully recognized in England ; and yet no Englishman of our time, not even De Quincey, has done any prose imaginative work to be named with theirs. But in comparing Poe with Hawthorne, we see that the genius of the latter has hands and feet as well as wings, so that all his work is solid as masonry, while Poe's is broken and disfigured by all sorts of inequalities and imitations ; he not disdaining, for want of true integrity, to disguise and falsify, to claim knowledge that he did not possess, to invent quotations and references, and even, as Griswold showed, to manipulate and exaggerate puffs of himself. I remember the chagrin with which I looked through Tieck, in my student-days, to find the "Journey into the Blue Distance" to which Poe refers in the "House of Usher ; " and how one of the poet's intimates laughed me to scorn for being deceived by any of Poe's citations, saying that he hardly knew a word of German.

But, making all possible deductions, how wonderful remains the power of Poe's imaginative tales, and how immense is the ingenuity of his puzzles and disentanglements ! The conundrums of Wilkie

Collins never renew their interest after the answer
is known ; but Poe's can be read again and again.
It is where spiritual depths are to be touched, that
he shows his weakness ; where he attempts it, as in
"William Wilson," it seems exceptional ; where
there is the greatest display of philosophic form, he
is often most trivial, whereas Hawthorne is often
profoundest when he has disarmed you by his sim-
plicity. The truth is, that Poe lavished on things
comparatively superficial those great intellectual
resources which Hawthorne reverently husbanded
and used. That there is something behind even
genius to make or mar it, this is the lesson of the
two lives.

Poe makes one of his heroes define another as
"that *monstrum horrendum*, an unprincipled man
of genius." It is in the malice and fury of his own
critical work that his low moral tone most betrays
itself. No atmosphere can be more belittling than
that of his "New York Literati : " it is a mass of
vehement dogmatism and petty personalities ; opin-
ions warped by private feeling, and varying from
page to page. He seemed to have absolutely no
fixed standard of critical judgment, though it is true
that there was very little anywhere in America during
those acrimonious days, when the most honorable
head might be covered with insult or neglect,

while any young poetess who smiled sweetly on Poe or Griswold or Willis might find herself placed among the Muses. Poe complimented and rather patronized Hawthorne, but found him only "peculiar and *not* original;"[1] saying of him, "He has not half the material for the exclusiveness of literature that he has for its universality," whatever that may mean ; and finally he tried to make it appear that Hawthorne had borrowed from himself. He returned again and again to the attack on Longfellow as a wilful plagiarist, denouncing the trivial resemblance between his "Midnight Mass for the Dying Year" and Tennyson's "Death of the Old Year," as "belonging to the most barbarous class of literary piracy."[2] To make this attack was, as he boasted, "to throttle the guilty;"[3] and while dealing thus ferociously with Longfellow, thus condescendingly with Hawthorne, he was claiming a foremost rank among American authors for obscurities now forgotten, such as Mrs. Amelia B. Welby and Estelle Anne Lewis. No one ever did more than Poe to lower the tone of literary criticism in this country ; and the greater his talent, the greater the mischief.

As a poet he held for a time the place earlier

[1] Works, ed. 1853, III., 202.   [2] Works, ed. 1853, III., 325.
[3] III., 300.

occupied by Byron, and later by Swinburne, as the patron saint of all wilful boys suspected of genius, and convicted at least of its infirmities. He belonged to the melancholy class of wasted men, like the German Hoffman, whom perhaps of all men of genius he most resembled. No doubt, if we are to apply any standard of moral weight or sanity to authors, — a proposal which Poe would doubtless have ridiculed, — it can only be in a very large and generous way. If a career has only a manly ring to it, we can forgive many errors — as in reading, for instance, the autobiography of Benvenuto Cellini, carrying always his life in his hand amid a brilliant and reckless society. But the existence of a poor Bohemian, besotted when he has money, angry and vindictive when the money is spent, this is a dismal tragedy, for which genius only makes the footlights burn with more lustre. There is a passage in Keats's letters, written from the haunts of Burns, in which he expresses himself as filled with pity for the poet's life : " he drank with blackguards, he was miserable ; we can see horribly clear in the works of such a man his life, as if we were God's spies." Yet Burns's sins and miseries left his heart unspoiled, and this cannot be said of Poe. After all, the austere virtues — the virtues of Emerson, Hawthorne, Whittier — are the best soil for genius.

I like best to think of Poe as associated with his betrothed, Sarah Helen Whitman, whom I saw sometimes in her later years. That gifted woman had outlived her early friends and loves and hopes, and perhaps her literary fame, such as it was : she had certainly outlived her recognized ties with Poe, and all but his memory. There she dwelt in her little suite of rooms, bearing youth still in her heart and in her voice, and on her hair also, and in her dress. Her dimly-lighted parlor was always decked, here and there, with scarlet ; and she sat, robed in white, with her back always turned to the light, thus throwing a discreetly tinted shadow over her still thoughtful and noble face. She seemed a person embalmed while still alive : it was as if she might dwell forever there, prolonging into an indefinite future the tradition of a poet's love ; and when we remembered that she had been Poe's betrothed, that his kisses had touched her lips, that she still believed in him and was his defender, all criticism might well, for her sake, be disarmed, and her saintly life atone for his stormy and sad career.

THOREAU.

THERE is no fame more permanent than that which begins its real growth after the death of an author; and such is the fame of Thoreau. Before his death he had published but two books, " A Week on the Concord and Merrimack Rivers," and " Walden." Four more have since been printed, besides a volume of his letters and two biographies. One of these last appeared within a year or two in England, where he was, up to the time of his death, absolutely unknown. Such things are not accidental or the result of whim, and they indicate that the literary fame of Thoreau is secure. Indeed, it has already survived two of the greatest dangers that can beset reputation, — a brilliant satirist for a critic, and an injudicious friend for a biographer.

Both admirer and censor, both Channing in his memoir, and Lowell in his well-known criticism, have brought the eccentricities of Thoreau into undue prominence, and have placed too little stress on the vigor, the good sense, the clear perceptions, of the man. I have myself walked, talked, and corresponded with him, and can testify that the impression given by both these writers is far removed from that ordinarily made by Thoreau himself. While tinged here and there, like most New England thinkers of his time, with the manner of Emerson, he was yet, as a companion, essentially original, wholesome, and enjoyable. Though more or less of a humorist, nursing his own whims, and capable of being tiresome when they came uppermost, he was easily led away from them to the vast domains of literature and nature, and then poured forth endless streams of the most interesting talk. He taxed the patience of his companions, but not more so, on the whole, than is done by many other eminent talkers when launched upon their favorite themes.

It is hard for one who thus knew him to be quite patient with Lowell in what seems almost wanton misrepresentation. Lowell applies to Thoreau the word " indolent : " but you might as well speak of the indolence of a self-registering thermometer; it does not go about noisily, yet it never knows an idle moment. Lowell says that Thoreau " looked with utter contempt on the august drama of destiny, of which his country was the scene, and on

which the curtain had already risen ; "[1] but was it
Thoreau, or Lowell, who found a voice when the
curtain fell, after the first act of that drama, upon
the scaffold of John Brown?   Lowell accuses him
of a " seclusion which keeps him in the public
eye," and finds something " delightfully absurd " in
his addressing six volumes under such circumstances to the public, when the fact is that four of
these volumes were made up by friends, after Thoreau's death, from his manuscripts, or from his
stray papers in newspapers and magazines. Lowell
accepts throughout the popular misconception —
and has, indeed, done much to strengthen it — that
Thoreau hated civilization, and believed only in
the wilderness ; whereas Thoreau defined his own
position on this point with exceeding clearness, and
made it essentially the same with that of his critics.
" For a permanent residence it seemed to me that
there could be no comparison between this [Con-
cord] and the wilderness, necessary as the latter is
for a resource and a background, the raw material
of all our civilization. The wilderness is simple
almost to barrenness.   The partially cultivated
country it is which chiefly has inspired, and will
continue to inspire, the strains of poets such as
compose the mass of any literature."[2]

<hr />

[1] My Study Windows, p. 206.   [2] Maine Woods, p. 159: written in 1846.

Seen in the light of such eminently sensible remarks as these, it will by and by be discovered
that Thoreau's whole attitude has been need-
lessly distorted. Lowell says that "his shanty-
life was mere impossibility, so far as his own
conception of it goes, as an entire independency
of mankind. The tub of Diogenes had a sounder
bottom."[1] But what a man of straw is this that
Lowell is constructing! What is this "shanty-
life"? A young man living in a country village,
and having a passion for the minute observation of
nature, and a love for Greek and Oriental reading,
takes it into his head to build himself a study, not
in the garden or the orchard, but in the woods, by
the side of a lake. Happening to be poor, and to
live in a time when social experiments are in vogue
at Brook Farm and elsewhere, he takes a whimsical
satisfaction in seeing how cheaply he can erect his
hut, and afterwards support himself by the labor of
his hands.. He is not really banished from the
world, nor does he seek or profess banishment:
indeed, his house is not two miles from his mother's
door; and he goes to the village every day or two,
by his own showing, to hear the news.[2] In this
quiet abode he spends two years, varied by an
occasional excursion into the deeper wilderness at a

---

[1] My Study Windows, p. 208.   [2] Walden, p. 181.

distance. He earns an honest living by gardening
and land-surveying, makes more close and delicate
observations on nature than any other American
has ever made, and writes the only book yet written
in America, to my thinking, that bears an annual
perusal. Can it be really true that this is a life so
wasted, so unpardonable?

The artist LaFarge built himself a studio as bare
as Thoreau's and almost as lonely, among the Para-
dise Rocks, near Newport, and used to withdraw
from the fashionable summer world to that safe
retreat. Lowell himself has celebrated in immor-
tal verse the self-seclusion of Professor Gould,
who would lock himself into his Albany observa-
tory, and leave his indignant trustees to "admire
the keyhole's contour grand" from without. Is
the naturalist's work so much inferior to the artist's, — are the stars of thought so much less important than those of space, — that LaFarge and Gould
are to be praised for their self-devotion, and yet
Thoreau is to be held up to all coming time as
selfish? For my own part, with "Walden" in my
hands, I wish that every other author in America might try the experiment of two years in a
"shanty."

Let me not seem to do injustice to Lowell, who
closes his paper on Thoreau with a generous tribute

that does much to redeem his earlier injustice. The truth is, that Thoreau shared the noble protest against worldliness of what is called the " transcendental " period, in America, and naturally shared some of the intellectual extravagances of that seething time ; but he did not, like some of his contemporaries, make his whims an excuse for mere selfishness, and his home life—always the best test—was thoroughly affectionate and faithful. His lifelong celibacy was due, if I have been correctly informed, to an early act of lofty self-abnegation toward his own brother, whose love had taken the same direction with his own. Certainly his personal fortitude amid the privations and limitations of his own career was nothing less than heroic. There is nothing finer in literary history than his description, in his unpublished diary, of receiving from his publisher the unsold copies — nearly the whole edition — of his " Week on the Concord and Merrimack Rivers," and of his carrying the melancholy burden up-stairs on his shoulders to his study. " I have now a library," he says, " of nearly nine hundred volumes, over seven hundred of which I wrote myself." [1]

It will always be an interesting question, how far

[1] By the kindness of my friend H. G. O. Blake, Esq., of Worcester, Mass., the custodian of Thoreau's manuscripts, I am enabled to print this entire passage at the end of this chapter.

Thoreau's peculiar genius might have been modified or enriched by society or travel. In his diary he expresses gratitude to Providence, or, as he quaintly puts it, " to those who have had the handling of me," that his life has been so restricted in these directions, and that he has thus been compelled to extract its utmost nutriment from the soil where he was born. Yet in examining these diaries, even more than in reading his books, one is led to doubt, after all, whether this mental asceticism was best for him, just as one suspects that the vegetable diet in which he exulted may possibly have shortened his life. A larger experience might have liberalized some of his judgments, and softened some of his verdicts. He was not as just to men as to woodchucks ; and his " simplify, I say, simplify," might well have been relaxed a little for mankind, in view of the boundless affluence of external nature. The world of art might also have deeply influenced him, had the way been opened for its closer study. Emerson speaks of " the raptures of a citizen arrived at his first meadow ; " but a deep, ascetic soul like Thoreau's could hardly have failed to be touched to a far profounder emotion by the first sight of a cathedral.

The impression that Thoreau was but a minor Emerson will in time pass away, like the early class-

ification of Emerson as a second-hand Carlyle.
All three were the children of•their time, and had
its family likeness; but Thoreau had the *lumen sic-
cum*, or "dry light," beyond either of the others;
indeed, beyond all men of his day. His tempera-
ment was like his native air in winter, — clear, frosty,
inexpressibly pure and bracing. His power of literary appreciation was something marvellous, and
his books might well be read for their quotations,
like the sermons of Jeremy Taylor. His daring
imagination ventured on the delineation of just
those objects in nature which seem most defiant of
description, as smoke, mist, haze; and his three
poems on these themes have an exquisite felicity of
structure such as nothing this side of the Greek
anthology can equal. Indeed, the value of the
classic languages was never better exemplified than
in their influence on his training. They were real
"humanities" to him; linking him with the great
memories of the race, and with high intellectual
standards, so that he could never, like some of his
imitators, treat literary art as a thing unmanly and
trivial. His selection of points in praising his
favorite books shows this discrimination. He loves
to speak of "the elaborate beauty and finish, and
the lifelong literary labors of the ancients . . .
works as refined, as solidly done, and as beautiful

almost, as the morning itself." [1]   I remember how
that fine old classical scholar, the late John Glen
King, of Salem, used to delight in Thoreau as being
/ "the only man who thoroughly loved both nature
and Greek."

Thoreau died at forty-four, without having
achieved fame or fortune.   It is common to speak
of his life as a failure ; but to me it seems, with all
its drawbacks, to have been a great and eminent
success.   Even testing it only by the common appe-
tite of authors for immortality, his seems already a
sure and enviable place.   Time is rapidly melting
away the dross from his writings, and exhibiting
their gold.   But his standard was higher than the
mere desire for fame, and he has told it plainly.
"There is nowhere recorded," he complains, "a
simple and irrepressible satisfaction with the gift of
life, any memorable praise of God. . . . If the day
and the night are such that you greet them with joy,
and life emits a fragrance, like flowers and sweet-
scented herbs, — is more elastic, starry, and immor-
tal, — that is your success." [2]

NOTE. — The following passage is now first published,
from Thoreau's manuscript diary, the date being Oct. 28,
1853 : —
    "For a year or two past, my publisher, Munroe, has been

---

[1] Walden, p. 113.   [2] Walden, pp. 85, 233.

writing from time to time to ask what disposition should be made of the copies of 'A Week on the Concord and Merrimack Rivers,' still on hand, and àt last suggesting that he had use for the room they occupied in his cellar. So I had them all sent to me here; and they have arrived to-day by express, piling the man's wagon, seven hundred and six copies out of an edition of one thousand, which I bought of Munroe four years ago, and have been ever since paying for, and have not quite paid for yet. The wares are sent to me at last, and I have an opportunity to examine my purchase. They are something more substantial than fame, as my back knows, which has borne them up two flights of stairs to a place similar to that to which they trace their origin. Of the remaining two hundred ninety and odd, seventy-five were given away, the rest sold. I have now a library of nearly nine hundred volumes, over seven hundred of which I wrote myself. Is it not well that the author should behold the fruits of his labor? My works are piled up in my chamber, half as high as my head, my *opera omnia*. This *is* authorship. These are the work of my brain. There was just one piece of good luck in the venture. The unbound were tied up by the printer four years ago in stout paper wrappers, and inscribed, 'H. D. Thoreau's Concord River, fifty copies.' So Munroe had only to cross out ' River,' and write ' Mass.,' and deliver them to the expressman at once. I can see now what I write for, and the result of my labors. Nevertheless, in spite of this result, sitting beside the inert mass of my works, I take up my pen to-night to record what thought or experience I may have had, with as much satisfaction as ever. Indeed, I believe that this result is more inspiring and better than if a thousand had bought my wares. It affects my privacy less, and leaves me freer."

HOWELLS.

IT has perhaps been a misfortune to Mr. Howells, that in his position of editor of "The Atlantic Monthly " he has inevitably been shielded from
much of that healthful discussion which is usually
needed for the making of a good author. Sir
Arthur Helps says, that, if ordinary criticism gives
us little, it is still worth having : if it is not marked
by common sense, it still brings to us the common
nonsense, which is quite as important. But the
conductor of the leading literary magazine of a
nation is very apt to escape this wholesome ordeal.
Delicacy of course forbids his admitting any men-
tion of himself, whether for praise or blame, within
his own pages. Moreover, his leading literary contemporaries are also his contributors ; and for them
to discuss him freely, even elsewhere, is like publicly
debating the character of one's habitual host. Compare the position, in this respect, of Mr. Howells
and Mr. Henry James, Jr. Their writings are equally conspicuous before the community ; their merits

are equally marked, and so also are their demerits, real or attributed; yet what, a difference in the amount of criticism awarded to each! Each new book by Mr. Howells is received with an almost monotonous praise, as if it had no individuality, no salient points; while each story by Mr. James is debated through and through the newspapers, as if it were a fresh Waverley novel. I see no reason for this difference, except that Mr. Howells edits "The Atlantic Monthly," and that all other American writers are, as it were, sitting at his table, or wishing themselves there. He must himself regret this result, for he is too essentially an artist not to prize honest and faithful criticism; and it is almost needless to say that his career as an author has been thoroughly modest and free from all the arts of self-praise.

The peculiar charm of his prose style has also, doubtless, had its effect in disarming criticism. He rarely fails to give pleasure by the mere process of writing, and this is much, to begin with; just as, when we are listening to conversation, a musical voice gratifies us almost more than wit or wisdom. Mr. Howells is without an equal in America — and therefore without an equal among his English-speaking contemporaries — as to some of the most attractive literary graces. He has no rival in half-

tints, in modulations, in subtile phrases that touch
the edge of an assertion and yet stop short of it.
He is like a skater who executes a hundred graceful
curves within the limits of a pool a few yards square.
Miss Austen, the novelist, once described her art as
a little bit of ivory, on which she produced small
effect after much labor. She underrated her own
skill, as the comparison in some respects underrates
that of Howells; but his field is — or has until
lately seemed to be — the little bit of ivory.

This is attributing to him only what he has been
careful to claim for himself. He tells his methods
very frankly, and his first literary principle has been
to look away from great passions, and rather to ele-
vate the commonplace by minute touches. Not
only does he prefer this, but he does not hesitate to
tell us sometimes, half jestingly, that it is the only
thing to do. "As in literature the true artist will
shun the use even of real events if they are of an
improbable character, so the sincere observer of
man will not desire to look upon his heroic or occasional phases, but will seek him in his habitual
moods of vacancy and tiresomeness."[1] He may
not mean to lay this down as a canon of universal
authority, but he accepts it himself; and he accepts
with it the risk involved of a too-limited and micro-

---

[1] Their Wedding Journey, p. 86.

scopic range. That he has finally escaped this peril, is due to the fact that his method went, after all, deeper than he admitted : he was not merely a good-natured observer, like Geoffrey Crayon, Gentleman, but he had thoughts and purposes, something to protest against, and something to say.

He is often classed with Mr. James as representing the international school of novelists, yet in reality they belong to widely different subdivisions. After all, Mr. James has permanently set up his easel in Europe, Mr. Howells in America ; and the latter has been, from the beginning, far less anxious to compare Americans with Europeans than with one another. He is international only if we adopt Mr. Emerson's saying, that Europe stretches to the Alleghanies. As a native of Ohio, transplanted to Massachusetts, he never can forego the interest implied in this double point of view. The Europeanized American, and, if we may so say, the Americanized American, are the typical figures that re-appear in his books. Even in "The Lady of the Aroostook," although the voyagers reach the other side at last, the real contrast is found on board ship ; and, although his heroine was reared in a New-England village, he cannot forego the satisfaction of having given her California for a birthplace. Mr. James writes "international episodes : "

Mr. Howells writes inter-oceanic episodes : his best scenes imply a dialogue between the Atlantic and Pacific slopes.

It was long expected that there would appear some sequel to his " Chance Acquaintance." Bostonians especially wished to hear more of Miles Arbuton : they said, " It is impossible to leave a man so well-dressed in a situation so humiliating." But the sequel has, in reality, come again and again ; the same theme re-appears in " Out of the Question," in " The Lady of the Aroostook ; " it will re-appear while Mr. Howells lives. He is really contributing important studies to the future organization of our society. How is it to be stratified? How much weight is to be given to intellect, to character, to wealth, to antecedents, to inheritance? Not only must a republican nation meet and solve these problems, but the solution is more assisted by the writers of romances than by the compilers of statistics. Fourth of July orators cannot even state the problem : it almost baffles the finest touch. As, in England, you may read every thing ever written about the Established Church, and yet, after all, if you wish to know what a bishop or a curate is, you must go to Trollope's novels, so, to trace American " society " in its formative process, you must go to Howells ; he alone shows you the es-

sential forces in action. He can philosophize well
enough on the subject, as ₎where he points out
that hereditary wealth in America as yet represents
" nothing in the world, no great culture, no political
influence, no civic aspiration, not even a pecuniary
force, nothing but a social set, an alien club life,
a tradition of dining." [1] But he is not at heart a
philosopher ; he is a novelist, which is better, and
his dramatic situations recur again and again to the
essential point.

It is this constant purpose which gives dignity
and weight to his American delineations, even
where he almost wantonly checks himself and dis-
appoints us. Were he merely, as some suppose, a
skilful miniature-painter of young girls at watering-
places, his sphere would be very circumscribed.
At times he seems tempted to yield to this limita-
tion — during his brief foray into the path of short
dramatic sketches, for instance. These sketches
provoked comparison with innumerable French trifles, which they could not rival in execution. " Private Theatricals " offers the same thing on a larger
scale, and under still greater disadvantages. Mrs.
Farrell reveals herself, at the first glance, as a
coquette too shallow and vulgar to be really interesting ; and she never rises above that level until

[1] Their Wedding Journey, p. 69.

she disappears from the scene, flinging her last net for the cow-boy in the pasture. Her habit of flirting is a garment deliberately put on, an armor that creaks in the wearing. But if you wish to see how a Frenchman draws a coquette, read " Le Fiancé de Mlle. St. Maur," by Cherbuliez. The coquetry of Mme. d'Arolles is always round her as an atmosphere, intangible, all-embracing, fold within fold ; she coquets even with a rudimentary organ in herself that might be called her conscience ; and then, besides this enveloping atmosphere, she wears always a thin garment of social refinement that seems to shield her even when the last shred of decorum is about to drop. She is a thoroughly artistic creation ; in watching her never so closely, you cannot see the wires pulled ; but in " Private Theatricals " we seem constantly to have notice given, " Please observe, Mrs. Farrell is about to attitudinize ! "

The moral of all this is, that Mr. Howells cannot be, if he would, an artist *per se*, like Droz, in reading whose brilliant trifles we are in a world where the execution is all, the thought nothing, and the moral less than nothing. Nor does he succeed, like Thackeray, in making a novel attractive without putting a single agreeable character into it : Thackeray barely accomplished this in " Vanity

Fair ; " Mr. Howells was far less successful in the
most powerful and least satisfactory of all his books,
" A Foregone Conclusion." The greatest step he
has ever taken, both in popularity and in artistic
success, has been won by trusting himself to a generous impulse, and painting in " The Lady of the
Aroostook " a character worth the pains of describing. The book is not, to my thinking, free from
faults : the hero poses and proses, and the drunken
man is so realistic as to be out of place and over-
done ; but the character of the heroine seems to
me the high-water mark of Mr. Howells. It has
been feared that he would always remain the charm-
ing delineator of people who were, after all, under-
sized, — heroes and heroines like the little *figurines*
from Tanagra, or the admirable miniature groups
of John Rogers. He has now allowed himself a
bolder sweep of arm, a more generous handling of
full-sized humanity ; and with this work begins,
we may fain believe, the maturity of his genius.

HELEN JACKSON. ("H. H.")

M'LLE DE MONTPENSIER, grand-daughter of Henri Quatre, is said to have been " so famous in history that her name never appears in it;" she being known only as "La Grande Mademoiselle." This anonymousness may help the fame of a princess, but it must hurt that of an author. The initials " L. E. L.," so familiar to some of us in childhood, stood for a fame soon forgotten ; and this not so much because her poetry was weak, but because her name was in a manner nameless. However popular might be the poems of " H. H.," they were still attached to a rather vague and formless personality so long as these initials only were given ; to combine with this the still remoter individuality of "Saxe Holm," was only to deepen the sense of vagueness ; and if all the novels of the " No Name " series, instead of two of them, had been attributed to the same shadowy being, every one would have pronounced the suggestion quite credible. To take these various threads of mystery,

and weave them into a substantial fame, this passed
the power of public admiration. At any rate, an
applause so bewildered could hardly be heard across
the Atlantic ; and it is almost exasperating to find
that in England, for instance, where so many feeble
American reputations have been revived only to
die, there are few critics who know even the name
of the woman who has come nearest in our day and
tongue to the genius of Elizabeth Barrett Browning,
and who has made Christina Rossetti and Jean
Ingelow appear but second-rate celebrities.

When some one asked Emerson a few years
since whether he did not think " H. H." the best
woman-poet on this continent, he answered in his
meditative way, " Perhaps we might as well omit
the *woman ;* " thus placing her, at least in that moment's impulse, at the head of all. He used to cut
her poems from the newspapers as they appeared,
to carry them about with him, and to read them
aloud. His especial favorites were the most con-
densed and the deepest, those having something of
that kind of obscurity which Coleridge pronounced
to be a compliment to the reader. His favorite
among them all is or was the sonnet entitled

"THOUGHT.

"O Messenger, art thou the king, or I ?
  Thou dalliest outside the palace-gate
  Till on thine idle armor lie the late
  And heavy dews : the morn's bright, scornful eye
  Reminds thee; then, in subtle mockery,
  Thou smilest at the window where I wait
  Who bade thee ride for life. In empty state
  My days go on, while false hours prophesy
  Thy quick return; at last in sad despair
  I cease to bid thee, leave thee free as air ;
  When lo I thou stand'st before me glad and fleet,
  And lay'st undreamed-of treasures at my feet.
  Ah I messenger, thy royal blood to buy,
  I am too poor. Thou art the king, not I."[1]

The uncontrollableness of thought by will has never been better expressed by words than in this sonnet ; and there are others which utter emotion so profoundly, and yet with such artistic quiet, that each brief poem seems the summary of a life. Take this, for instance, describing a love that, having once found its shore, burns its ships behind it, and absolutely cuts off all retreat : —

"BURNT SHIPS.

"O Love, sweet Love, who came with rosy sail
  And foaming prow across the misty sea I
  O Love, brave Love, whose faith was full and free

[1] Verses by H. H., p. 121.

That lands of sun and gold which could not fail
Lay in the west, — that bloom no wintry gale
Could blight, and eyes whose love thine own should be,
Called thee with steadfast voice of prophecy
To shores unknown !

         " O Love, poor Love, avail
Thee nothing now thy faiths, thy braveries ;
There is no sun, no bloom ; a cold wind strips
The bitter foam from off the wave where dips
No more thy prow ; the eyes are hostile eyes ;
The gold is hidden ; vain thy tears and cries :
O Love, poor Love, why didst thou burn thy ships ? "[1]

    " H. H." writes another class of poems, that, with
a grace and wealth like Andrew Marvell's, carry us
into the very life of external nature, or link it with
the heart of man. Emerson's " Humblebee " is
not a creation more fresh and wholesome than is

"MY STRAWBERRY.

" O marvel, fruit of fruits, I pause
   To reckon thee. I ask what cause
   Set free so much of red from heats
   At core of earth, and mixed such sweets
   With sour and spice ; what was that strength
   Which out of darkness, length by length,
   Spun all thy shining thread of vine
   Netting the fields in bond as thine ;
   I see thy tendrils drink by sips
   From grass and clover's smiling lips ;

        [1] Verses, p. 71.

> I hear thy roots dig down for wells
> Tapping the meadow's hidden cells;
> Whole generations of green things,
> Descended from long lines of springs,
> I see make room for thee to bide
> A quiet comrade by their side;
> I see the creeping peoples go
> Mysterious journeys to and fro;
> Treading to right and left of thee,
> Doing thee homage wonderingly.
> I see the wild bees as they fare
> Thy cups of honey drink, but spare;
> I mark thee bathe and bathe again
> In sweet uncalendared spring rain.
> I watch how all May has of sun
> Makes haste to have thy ripeness done,
> While all her nights let dews escape
> To set and cool thy perfect shape.
> Ah, fruit of fruits, no more I pause
> To dream and seek thy hidden laws!
> I stretch my hand, and dare to taste
> In instant of delicious waste
> On single feast, all things that went
> To make the empire thou hast spent." [1]

As the most artistic among her verses I should class the "Gondolieds," in which all Venice seems reflected in the movement and cadence, while the thought is fresh and new and strong. Then there are poems which seem to hold all secrets of pas-

[1] Verses, p. 166.

sion trembling on the lips, yet forbear to tell them; and others, on a larger scale, which have a grander rhythmical movement than most of our poets have dared even to attempt. Of these the finest, to my ear, is "Resurgam;" but I remember that Charlotte Cushman preferred the "Funeral March," and loved to read it in public. Those who heard her can never forget the solemnity with which she recited those stately cadences, or the grandeur of her half-glance over the shoulder as she named first among the hero's funeral attendants

"Majestic Death, his freedman, following."

"H. H." reaches the popular heart best in a class of poems easy to comprehend, thoroughly human in sympathy; poems of love, of motherhood, of bereavement; poems such as are repeated and preserved in many a Western cabin, cheering and strengthening many a heart. Other women have exerted a similar power; but in the hands of a writer like Alice Cary, for instance, the influence is shallow, though pure and wholesome; she sounds no depths as this later poet sounds them. The highest type of this class of Helen Jackson's verses may be found in the noble poem entitled "Spinning," which begins: —

> " Like a blind spinner in the sun
>   I tread my days ;
> I know that all the threads will run
>   Appointed ways ;
> I know each day will bring its task,
> And, being blind, no more I ask."[1]

No finer symbolic picture of human life has ever been framed : Henry Vaughan, had he been a woman, might have written it.

If, in addition to her other laurels, Mrs. Jackson is the main author of the "Saxe Holm" tales, she must be credited not only with some of the very best stories yet written in America, — " Draxy Miller's Dowry," for instance, — but with one of the best-kept of all literary secrets.   There has been something quite dramatic in the skill with which the puzzle has been kept alive by the appearance of imaginary claimants — if imaginary they be — to the honor of this authorship : now a maiden lady in the interior of New York ; now a modest young girl whose only voucher, Celia Burleigh, died without revealing her name.   I do not know whether any of these claimants took the pains to write out whole stories in manuscript, — as an Irish pretender copied out whole chapters of Miss Edgeworth's " Castle Rackrent," with corrections and erasures,

---

[1] Verses, p. 14.

— but it is well known that the editors of "Scrib-
ner's Monthly" were approached by some one who
professed to have dropped the "Saxe Holm" stories in the street, and demanded that they should
be restored to him. He was suppressed by the
simple expedient of inviting him to bring in some
specimens of his own poetry, that it might be com-
pared with that of "Draxy Miller;" but the modest young girls and the apocryphal rural contributors were less easily abolished, though time has
abated their demands. The more Mrs. Jackson
denied the authorship, the more resolutely the public mind intrenched itself in the belief that she had
something to do with the stories, and that at least
the verses therein contained were hers and hers
alone. There were coincidences of personal and
local details, to connect her with the veiled author;
and the fantastic title of one tale, "The One-
legged Dancers," had previously appeared in her
"Bits of Travel."[1] The final verdict seemed to be
that she must have written the books, with enough
of aid from some friend to justify her persistent
denial; and ingenious critics soon began to see
internal traces of a double authorship, while this
to other critics seemed altogether absurd.

The publication of "Mercy Philbrick's Choice"

[1] Bits of Travel, p. 65.

and " Hetty's Strange History " only revived the
same questions.   The plots of these books showed
the hand of " Saxe Holm," the occasional verses
that of " H. H." Both novels brought a certain dis-
appointment : they had obvious power, but were too
painful to be heartily enjoyed.   After all, the public
mind is rather repelled by a tragedy, since people
wish to be made happy.   Great injustice has been
done by many critics, I think, to " Hetty's Strange
History."   While its extraordinary power is con-
ceded, it has been called morbid and immoral ; yet
it is as stern a tale of retribution as " Madame
Bovary " or "The Scarlet Letter." We rarely find
in fiction any severity of injustice meted out to a
wrong act done from noble motives.   In Jean
Paul's " Siebenkäs " the husband feigns death in
order that his wife may find happiness without him :
he succeeds in his effort, and is at last made happy
himself.   In " Hetty's Strange History " the wife
effaces herself with precisely the same object, — for
her husband's sake : but the effort fails ; the husband is not made happy by her absence, and when
they are re-united the memory of her deception
cannot be banished, so that after the first bliss of
re-union they find that complete healing can never
come.   Only a deep nature could have planned,

only a very firm pen could have traced, the final punishment of Hetty's sin.

One of the acutest critics in America said of Saxe Holm: "She stands on the threshold of the greatest literary triumphs ever won by an American woman." It must be owned that she still lingers there: we still wait for any complete and unquestionable victory. Who knows but that versatile imagination may already have sought some other outlet, and she may already be mystifying her public under some new name? And of " H. H." as a poet it must be said that she seems of late to be half shrinking from her full career, and to be turning rather to the path of descriptive prose. She has always excelled in this: her "German Landlady" is unsurpassed in its way, and her new experiences of Western residence have only added fulness and finish to this part of her literary work. No one has ever written of frontier-life so well as she, in her " Bits of Travel at Home ;" with such hearty sympathy, with a tone so discriminating, and with such absence of the merely coarse or melodramatic. All the California writers have not secured for the life of that region such a place in the world of art as she is giving to Colorado ; all their work, however brilliant, is encumbered with what is crude, cheap, exaggerated, and therefore temporary ; hers is clear and firm and strong ; and those who regret her absence from her early home can yet rejoice that she dwells amid scenery so magnificent, and in so absorbing a current of human life.

HENRY JAMES, JR.

WE are growing more cosmopolitan and
varied, in these United States of America;
and our authors are gaining much, if they are also
losing a little, in respect to training. The early
career of an American author used to be tolerably
fixed and clear, if limited; a college education,
a few months in Europe, a few years in some
profession, and then an entrance into literature
by some side-door. In later times, the printing-
office has sometimes been substituted for the college, and has given a new phase of literary character distinct from the other, but not less valuable.
Mr. Henry James, Jr., belongs to neither of the
classes thus indicated: he may be said to have
been trained in literature by literature itself, so early
did he begin writing, and so incessantly has he written. We perhaps miss in his works something of
the method which the narrower classical nurture
was supposed to give; and we find few traces
of that contact with the mass of mankind which

comes through mere daily duty to the professional man, the business man, the journalist. Mr. James has kept a little too good company : we do not find in his books such refreshing types of hearty and robust manhood as Howells, with all his daintiness, finds it easy to depict in Colonel Ellison and the skipper of the Aroostook. Then Mr. James's life has been so far transatlantic, that one hardly knows whether he would wish to be accounted an American writer, after all ; so that his education, his point of view, his methods, all unite to place him in a class by himself.

It is pleasant to see a man write, as he has always done, with abundant energy, and seemingly from the mere love of writing. Yet it is impossible to deny that he has suffered from this very profusion. Much of his early work seems a sort of self-training, gained at the expense of his readers ; each sheet, each story, has been hurried into print before the ink was dry, in order to test it on the public, — a method singularly removed from the long and lonely maturing of Hawthorne. "*L'oisiveté est nécessaire aux esprits, aussi bien que le travail.*" Even the later books of Mr. James, especially his travels and his essays, show something of this defect. What a quarry of admirable suggestions is, for instance, his essay on Balzac ;

but how prolix it is, what repetitions, what a want of condensation and method! The same is true, in a degree, of his papers on George Sand and Turgénieff, while other chapters in his "French Poets and Novelists" are scarcely more than sketches : the paper on the *Théâtre Français* hardly mentions Sarah Bernhardt ; and, indeed, that on Turgénieff says nothing of his masterpiece, "Terres Vierges." Through all these essays he shows delicacy, epigram, quickness of touch, penetration ; but he lacks symmetry of structure, and steadiness of hand.

We can trace in the same book, also, some of the author's limitations as an imaginative artist, since in criticising others a man shows what is wanting in himself. When he says, for instance, that a monarchical society is "more available for the novelist than any other," he shows that he does not quite appreciate the strong point of republicanism, in that it develops real individuality in proportion as it diminishes conventional distinctions. The truth is, that the modern novel has risen with the advance of democratic society, on the ruins of feudalism. Another defect is seen from time to time, when, in criticising some well-known book, he misses its special points of excellence. Take, for instance, his remarks on that masterly and repulsive novel, "Madame Bovary." To say of the author of that work that his "theory as a novelist, briefly expressed, is to begin at the outside," [1] seems almost whimsically unjust. There is not a character in modern fiction developed more essentially from within than that of this heroine : all her sins and sorrows are virtually predicted in the early chapters ; even Mr. James has to admit that it "could not have been otherwise" [2] with her, thereby taking back his own general assertion. Then he says "every thing in the book is ugly," [3] whereas one of its salient points is the beauty of the natural descriptions in which its most painful incidents are framed. Finally, — and this is the most puzzling misconception of all, — Mr. James utterly fails to see the bearing of one of the pivotal points of the narrative, an unfortunate surgical operation performed by the heroine's husband, a country doctor : he calls it an "artistic bravado," [3] and treats it as a mere episode of doubtful value, whereas it is absolutely essential to the working-out of the plot. The situation is this : Madame Bovary is being crushed to the earth by living in a social vacuum, with a stupid husband whom she despises, and has already deceived. She has just felt a

---

[1] French Poets and Novelists, p. 256.   [2] Ibid., p. 261.
[3] Ibid., p. 265.

twinge of remorse, after receiving an affectionate
letter from her father; when suddenly this commonplace husband is presented to her eyes in a
wholly new light, — that of an unappreciated man of
genius, who has by a single act won a place among
the great surgeons of his time. All that is left
undepraved in her nature is touched and roused by
this: she will do any thing, bear any thing, for
such a husband. The illusion lasts but a few days,
and is pitilessly torn away : the husband proves a
mere vulgar, ignorant quack, even duller, emptier,
more hopeless, than she had dreamed. The re-
action takes her instantly downward, and with that
impulse she sinks to rise no more. The author
himself (Flaubert) takes the pains to warn us distinctly beforehand of the bearing of this inci-
dent ; [1] but his precaution seems needless, the thing
explains itself. It is one of the strongest and
clearest passages in the whole tragedy, and it seems
as if there must be some defect of artistic sensibility
in any critic who misses his way here. Or else —
which is more probable — it is another instance of
that haste in literary workmanship which is one
of Mr. James's besetting sins.

---

[1] " *Elle demeurait fort embarrassée dans sa velléité de sacrifice,
quand l'apothécaire vint à propos lui fournir une occasion.*" —
MADAME BOVARY, p. 210.

It may be one result of this extreme rapidity of
production, that Mr. James uses certain catch-words
so often as to furnish almost a shibboleth for his
style ; such words, for instance, as " brutal," " puer-
ile," " immense."   Another result is seen in his indifference to careful local coloring, especially where
the scene is laid in the United States.   When he
draws Americans in Europe, he is at home ; when
he brings Europeans across the Atlantic, he never
seems quite sure of his ground, except in Newport,
which is in some respects the least American spot
on this continent.   He opens his " Europeans " by
exhibiting horse-cars in the streets of Boston nearly
ten years before their introduction, and his whole
sketch of the Wentworth family gives a sense of
vagueness.   It is not difficult to catch a few unmis-
takable points, and portray a respectable elderly
gentleman reading " The Daily Advertiser ; " but
all beyond this is indefinite, and, when otherwise,
sometimes gives quite an incorrect impression of
the place and period described.   The family portrayed has access to " the best society in Boston ; "
yet the daughter, twenty-three years old, has " never
seen an artist," though the picturesque figure of
Allston had but lately disappeared from the streets,
at the time mentioned, and Cheney, Staigg, and
Eastman Johnson might be seen there any day, with

plenty of other artists less known. The household
is perfectly amazed and overwhelmed at the sight of
two foreigners, although there probably were more
cultivated Europeans in Boston thirty years ago than
now, having been drawn thither by the personal
celebrity or popularity of Agassiz, Ticknor, Longfellow, Sumner, and Dr. Howe. The whole picture —
though it is fair to remember that the author calls it
a sketch only — seems more like a delineation of
American society by Fortunio or Alexandre Dumas
fils, than like a portraiture by one to the manor born.
The truth is, that Mr. James's cosmopolitanism is,
after all, limited : to be really cosmopolitan, a man
must be at home even in his own country.

There are no short stories in our recent literature, I think, which are so good as Mr. James's
best, — "Madame de Mauves," for instance, and
"The Madonna of the Future." Even these sometimes lack condensation ; but they have a thoroughly original grasp, and fine delineations of character. It is a great step downward from these to
the somewhat vulgar horrors contained in "A
Romance of Certain Old Clothes." The author
sometimes puts on a cynicism which does not go
very deep ; and the young lovers of his earlier tales
had a disagreeable habit of swearing at young
ladies, and ordering them about. Yet he has kept

himself very clear from the disagreeable qualities of the French fiction he loves. His books never actually leave a bad taste in one's mouth, as Charlotte Brontë said of French novels ; and, indeed, no one has touched with more delicate precision the vexed question of morality in art. He finely calls the longing after a moral ideal "this southern slope of the mind,"[1] and says of the ethical element, " It is in reality simply a part of the richness of inspiration : it has nothing to do with the artistic process, and it has every thing to do with the artistic effect."[2] This is admirable ; and it is a vindication of this attribute when we find that Mr. James's most successful social stories, "An International Episode," and " Daisy Miller," have been written with distinct purpose, and convey lessons. He has achieved no greater triumph than when, in this last-named book, he succeeds in holding our sympathy and even affection, after all, for the essential innocence and rectitude of the poor wayward girl whose follies he has so mercilessly portrayed.

It cannot be said that Mr. James has yet succeeded in producing a satisfactory · novel : as a clever woman has said, he should employ some one else to write the last few pages. However strong the characterizations, however skilful the plot, the

---

[1] French Poets and Novelists, p. 114.   [2] Ibid., p. 82.

reader is left discontented. If in this respect he
seems behind Howells, it must be remembered that
James habitually deals with profounder emotions,
and is hence more liable to be overmastered.
Longfellow says to himself in his "Hyperion," "O
thou poor authorling! Reach a little deeper into
the human heart! Touch those strings, touch
those deeper strings more boldly, or the notes shall
die away like whispers, and no ear shall hear them
save thine own." It is James rather than Howells
who has heeded this counsel. The very disap-
pointment which the world felt at the close of
"The American" was in some sense a tribute to
its power : the author had called up characters and
situations which could not be cramped, at last,
within the conventional limits of a stage-ending.
As a piece of character-drawing, the final irresolu-
tion of the hero was simply perfect : it seemed one
of the cases where a romancer conjures up persons
who are actually alive, and who insist on working
out a destiny of their own, irrespective of his
wishes. To be thus conquered by one's own creation might seem one of those defeats that are
greater than victories ; yet it is the business of the
novelist, after all, to keep his visionary people well in
hand, and to contrive that they shall have their own
way, and yet not spoil his climax. In life, as in "The

American," the most complicated situations often
settle themselves by events unseen, and the most
promising tragedies are cheated of their crisis.   But
it is not enough that literary art should give a true
transcript of nature ; for the work must also com-
ply with the laws of art, and must have a beginning,
a middle, and an end.   " *Un ouvrage d'art doit
être un être, et non une chose arbitraire.*"[1]

[1] Pensées de J. Joubert, p. 289.

www.ingramcontent.com/pod-product-compliance
Lightning Source LLC
Chambersburg PA
CBHW022155020726
47496CB00008B/2722